I0158420

# FIVE SENSES OF SUCCESSFUL LEADERS

**NICHOLAS DLAMINI**

ii

**Copyright** @ Nicholas Dlamini 2022

All rights reserved, no part of this publication may be reproduced, stored in a retrieval system, or transmitted, in any form or by any means, electronic, mechanical, photocopying, recording, or otherwise, without the prior permission of the publishers.

Unless otherwise indicated all scripture quotation is from the New King James Version of the holy Bible.

FIVE SENSES OF SUCCESSFUL LEADERS

First print 2022

Published by

Graceworx Publishers

50 Modumbla Cul De Sac

Lotus Gardens

0008

ISBN: 978-0-6397-6028-5

**OTHER BOOKS BY THE SAME AUTHOR:**

*The Apostolic And Prophetic Prayer Manual*

*How To Operate In Secular Babylon*

# ACKNOWLEDGEMENTS

To my dear sister in the Lord, Sphiwe Faith Mashiye, your support towards my work is why I could do this publication. I celebrate you and your many words of encouragement, for standing beside me in all my endeavors, and for your candor whenever you disagree with me. Without you, I would not have been able to publish this work at all. Thank you so much, and may the Lord richly bless you.

# DEDICATION

*To my son Zipho and my daughter Jedidah, this is an investment into your lives and your future. May it help you to become great leaders in society and better versions of yourselves!*

# ENDORSEMENTS

Reading this book was like listening to someone speak directly to my core. What an awakening; the author speaks directly to his audience, just as the title states. I am encouraged and corrected in my way of thinking as a leader. Thank you for pouring out your wisdom and kindling the fire in my heart.

**Pastor Precious** assistant pastor at Agape Kingdom Dominion Church in Fort Dodge IA, USA. Farm manager at ACP LLC.

I am astonished at the wisdom that is in this book. I realize that the writing of this book is timely because we're in the season where God is preparing the church for wealth transfer. This book serves as an alarm clock to wake us up and use the necessary tools, namely, the five senses, to advance the kingdom mandate.

This book exposes our complacency as believers who depend solely on the supernatural senses (especially pastors) and not exploring other areas, such as the innovative sense. I believe this book will help the readers to discover their strong senses and those they need to improve on. I could say a lot, but I am grateful to have read this book; it has opened my eyes and motivated me to take risks that I thought were crazy.

I recommend it to everyone who aspires to be great; it is surely one of the best books I have read about leadership. Thank you, Apostle of Christ.

**Apostle Nelson Mohale**. *God of glory international ministries, Witbank, South Africa.*

In the book, 'The Five Senses Of Successful Leaders,' Nicholas Dlamini talks about the five leadership senses that every leader needs. I am personally challenged and impressed by how the author explains these leadership senses; the entrepreneurial sense mostly strikes me.

The author explains the importance of being an entrepreneurial leader. This is a sense that enables a leader to pioneer not only in business but other endeavors. One would be correct to say that all leaders in all spheres of life, including pastors, need this leadership sense. The author shows vividly that a leader with an entrepreneurial sense is a visionary and operates supernaturally.

One cannot wait to see the qualities of an entrepreneurial leader that the author narrates in this book. I recommend this book to leaders and those who are not in positions of leadership without any reservation. I give it a four-star rating.

**Reverend M.J. Mphego**. *Assemblies of God, Tweefontein South Africa.*

*5 Senses of successful leaders* is not just a book but an experience. The author's prolific writing style makes it hard to put the book down once you start reading. This book is a must-read for every leader, businessperson, and entrepreneur. The author's approach to describing the different senses is mind-blowing. I have four words to describe my reading experience so far: Permeative, Reminiscent, Powerful, and Evocative; such a great read.

**Dr Tina Magagula**. *Author of Christmas Without You.*

Firstly, the book's title gives two connotations, both secular and spiritual. One can mistake this book for a secular leadership book. Its definition gives the proper context from which the author writes. Some questions are answered through the proper and accurate definitions which are provided.

It is simple to read and understand yet thought provoking; it is power packed and answers various questions that one might ponder based on the book's outline. It is easy to understand from the onset, compared to some books which have narratives that are hard to digest, this one is easier. It's deep, yet the outline and chronology make you flow with the author's thought; one easily relates with what is written because of the simplicity and homiletical approach employed.

**Pastor Wandile Lumbiwa SG**. Alliance Church Phumula Branch.

Apostle Nicholas tackles the knotty inquiry on the multi-faceted dimensions of leadership. I'm glad he has made it easy for the 'fool' to comprehend and practice the laid-out propositions. Through this read, I was able to mirror myself and project. There will be a lot of troubleshooting and recalibration for those already in leadership, thus thrusting themselves into a deeper level of practical cognizance.

I have read books on leadership, but this one touched every fiber of my being, leaving me with this insatiable thirst and rapacious hunger to dig deeper into the subject. The author can capture the reader and inspire greatness.

**Prophet Sboking**. *Sound of Heaven, Kingdom of Eswatini.*

# CONTENTS

*Acknowledgments*

*Dedication*

*Endorsements*

**About The Author**

# PRELUDE

The soul is the divine spark that makes any inanimate object alive. It is the engine that drives every living being, from plants and animals to humans. There is nothing alive that has no soul. Simply put, every living thing has a soul. The soul transcends living organisms such as plants or mankind to organizations.

Everything that lives has a soul, whether a plant, animal, family, or organization. What makes an organization alive is the soul of that organization. Therefore, souls differ from one entity to another.

There is a soul of plants and that of animals. The scripture also tells us that God has a soul too (Hebrews 10:38). The soul of God is what makes Him who He is, an Omnipotent, Omniscient, and Omnipresent God. Because of His soul, He can boldly declare that "I am not a man nor the son of man...." He is not ashamed of that. Man has a soul too.

The soul is the seat of instinct and senses. When the soul departs from a particular body, that body loses its senses and therefore is pronounced dead, be it the body of a plant, animal, or man. The design of man's soul makes him more valuable to God than plants and animals. It is this soul that makes man eligible for judgment and rewards. There are five senses found in most animals and man's soul: sight, hearing, smell, touch, and taste. What sets man apart is that he also has five more senses. We call these senses spiritual senses. These senses are not from the soul but from the spirit of man, whereas animals do not have spirits.

The spiritual sense of sight is perception; the spiritual sense of hearing is understanding; the spiritual sense of smell is discernment/judgment; the spiritual sense of taste is choice (the ability to endorse or reject something); and the spiritual sense of touch is mood (the ability to be affected by what happens around that makes one happy, sad, angry etc.)

**The Soul Of Leaders**

We have already enumerated that the souls of living beings differ from one entity to the other. This book is not so much about the soul as we know it, but I have borrowed the term "soul" to elaborate on a point the Lord gave me about leadership.

Now, what is sense? Sense is the logic behind the meaning. When someone says, "This is not making sense," they mean they cannot find logic or meaning that sits well in their line of thought. Applying something that does not make sense to you is almost impossible.

Even the things of God are a form of logic or sense. They may not be common sense, but they are not nonsense.

There is no such thing called "nonsense." Nothing in this world is without sense. There are classes and levels of sense. One cannot make sense of one aspect of meaning. Meaning is broad and cannot be understood one-dimensionally.

Sense is the machine that tests logic before implementation. Therefore, there is no sense for sense or no meaning behind meaning. Without sense, there cannot be meaning; without meaning, there cannot be logic. This is what divides humans according to their classifications - sense.

What makes leaders special is their souls. The soul of leaders is different from the rest of the people. I will show you in this book the five classes of human beings based on the five senses that make a successful leader. A successful leader must have all five leadership senses. These senses make a leader's soul, which makes the leader stand out in society. Every successful leader must have a soul; otherwise, they will remain common.

# ONE

# COMMON SENSE

According to the Cambridge Dictionary common sense is the basic level of practical knowledge and judgment that we all need to help us live in a reasonable and safe way. Merriam Webster's Dictionary defines common sense as "sound and prudent judgment based on a simple perception of the situation or facts.

This is the ability to deduce by using the information that is available to you. For example, if a woman is married to an abusive husband, it is common sense to opt for divorce and not think that when God forbids divorce, He is also referring to these extreme situations.

Common sense is one's natural ability to make a sound judgment concerning practical matters. It is how we are all expected to view reality; for example, the sun rises in the East and sets in the West. That general understanding is common to all. A person lacking common sense is regarded as a fool or foolish.

This is the divine deposit that sets humans apart from animals. Animals operate on instinct, but humans use sense. Sense is the inner judge that gives a verdict concerning matters of life. It is given to all people, and they are all expected to possess some level thereof to make a sound judgment over practical matters.

This is the only judge that exposes fools. Although common sense is generally expected to be possessed by all people, it is a must-have for everyone who serves in leadership, be it in politics, religion, home, or business. Any leader who lacks common sense will violate sound judgment and do things that even common people do not do. In that case, it is safe to say that we have appointed a fool into leadership. Foolishness is a brain that lacks sound judgment; therefore, a fool is a lesser person in society. Fools never succeed at anything because their foolishness exposes them as lesser people, and no one wants to follow a lesser person.

Common sense or sound judgment also determines the maturity of a person. Depending on how much sound judgment a person lacks will determine how immature they are perceived to be. Maturity is the food for longevity in politics, sports, or leadership. The gift usually ushers you to success, but sound judgment sustains you.

Sound judgment is also the mother of character; it tells a person what and what not to say. Without sound judgment, many relationships will fail. A leader who lacks sound judgment lacks common sense and cannot lead successfully. He is somewhat juvenile and can become a stumbling block to his success and destiny.

In the Book of Ecclesiastes 10:16, 17 (KJV), the scripture says, "Woe to thee, O land, when thy king is a child, and thy princes eat in the morning! Blessed art thou, O land, when thy king is the son of nobles, and thy princes eat in due season, for strength, and not for drunkenness!" It reveals to us the state of mind of someone who lacks common sense. It likens such a person to a child and moans for those whom such a child leads.

It is dangerous to be led by someone who lacks common sense. The Bible calls such a person a fool. The Bible has a lot to say about fools. Here are some examples:

Pro 1:7 The fear of the LORD is the beginning of knowledge, but fools despise wisdom and instruction.

Pro 3:35 The wise shall inherit glory, but shame shall be the legacy of fools.

Pro 9:13 A foolish woman is clamorous; she is simple and knows nothing.

Pro 10:8 The wise in heart will receive commands, but a prating fool will fall.

Read also Proverbs

Psa_5:5; Psa_14:1; Psa_53:1; Psa_74:18-22; Psa_107:1 10:1; Pro_10:10; Pro_10:13; Pro_10:14; Pro_10:18; Pro_10:23; Pro_14:1; Pro_14:7-9; Pro_14:15; Pro_15:7; Pro_15:20; Pro_15:21; Pro_17:24; Pro_17:25; Pro_18:2; Pro_18:6; Pro_18:7; Pro_19:13; Pro_20:3; Pro_21:20; Pro_26:3-12; Pro_29:9; Pro_29:11; Ecc_4:5; Ecc_7:9; Ecc_10:11-15; Mat_7:26; Mat_7:27; Tit_3:3;

It is amazing how all these scriptures deal with common sense. The above scriptures teach that it is foolishness not to do the following:

- Fear God or live a godly life.
- Listen to advice.
- Believe in the existence of God. Amazingly, atheism is put in the category of foolishness in the scriptures.
- Do hard labor. Laziness is paralleled with foolishness.

- Obey God's Word and elders.
- Budget.
- Question things before believing them.
- Seek understanding before speaking or acting upon a matter.

A leader who lacks sound judgment is a disadvantage and a stumbling to himself and those he leads. The Bible deals with things leaders should not do because they would be considered foolish. The Book of Proverbs teaches that leaders should not drink alcohol. It puts it this way:

Pro 31:4, 5 It is not for kings, O Lemuel, It is not for kings to drink wine, Nor for princes intoxicating drink; Lest they drink and forget the law, And pervert the justice of all the afflicted.

Alcohol is associated with the difference between kings versus subjects, lords versus peasants, and the wise versus the foolish. Since alcohol clouds one's judgment, it is not for people who want to lead successfully. Once people consider you a fool, they will stop respecting you. Whether you are a pastor, a wife, a husband, or a mayor, you should not be considered a fool. Foolishness kills the desire for people to follow you.

### Things A Leader Should Avoid To Lead Well

The following points are life-changing once you see them in this light: prudence versus foolishness.

A lot that we claim to struggle with is not demonic, nor are we victims in the situation. The challenge we have today is foolishness. I am a living testimony that no matter who you are, you can struggle with foolishness. You can even think that you need prayer only to find that you need to stop being stupid.

I want you to sit back and think hard about the following points and see if you do not need to work on yourself and eliminate some of your life's stupidity.

## Sexual immorality and flirtation

Wise leaders flee fornication. I used to think that if I struggled with lust and sexual immorality, I needed some deliverance. I thought there must be some bloodline curse from which I needed to be free. I never considered the possibility that I did all that because I was foolish.

I learned as I grew in leadership that a man who cheats is foolish, not possessed. A person who flirts with other people of the opposite sex is foolish, not possessed. Pornography is foolishness, not just a demonic problem. We sometimes endorse foolishness and make it a prayer point. But the moment you see your foolishness, you will be empowered to want to change genuinely.

## Aggressive and abusive behavior

Being rude to people is also stupidity. Again, once you demonize your toxic character, you will always have someone or something to blame other than yourself. "The devil made me do it" mentality is an escapist attitude that does not want to take responsibility. Fools tend to act as victims.

Another problem is that we tend to spiritualize our bad behaviors and hide behind the façade of ministry and vocation. Many years ago, I used to be very rude on the pulpit. I would shout at people and embarrass others, and people were willing to accept that this was my vocation. However, I refused that position. I refused to remain bitter and uncool. I told myself that I would be a nice person. It took a while, but I can say I am no longer that man who was always rude.

Other people claim they are being honest and straightforward when they are rude. They hurt people and then say, "You got your feelings hurt because you hate being told the truth." However, this person is not honest; they are foolish.

A foolish woman stays with an abusive man, and it is foolish to tolerate an abusive environment. It is also wise to leave a fool. If you willingly stay with a fool, hoping they will change, you become a fool yourself.

## Foolish talk and silliness

Too much talk exposes one's immaturity. This is not to say that leaders should not laugh or tell jokes, but there is always a thin line between joking within limits and becoming a fool.

There are many funny videos nowadays on social media that we share on our platforms, especially on WhatsApp. However, we do not share everything funny; some things are foolish and endorsing them is to endorse stupidity. As a leader, you cannot be seen endorsing all sorts of foolishness on a public platform.

Leadership goes with some seriousness because people will not follow a fool. They will not follow someone they consider not worthy of respect and obedience. Therefore, it is wise to watch yourself as a leader and not be seen saying foolish things or endorsing folly.

# TWO

# ACQUIRED SENSE

According to Merriam Webster's Dictionary, to acquire is to come to have as a new or added characteristic, trait, or ability (as sustained by effort or natural selection). It also says that to acquire is to come to have something gradually. Acquired sense means that one can develop it through different means. This refers to intelligence.

Intelligence can be acquired, and a skill learned. You can acquire a certain skill set. This is what I call acquired sense. Leaders have acquired sense; they keep growing spiritually, psychologically, and experientially.

One thing you must learn as a leader is that anything that you can acquire, you can possess. Some skills are learned through application or by paying attention. Do not limit yourself to the level of knowledge you are in. There is a vast universe of knowledge in the world; all you need to do is acquire it.

## HOW TO DEVELOP ACQUIRED SENSE

### Through learning

Many things we have acquired through the years result from learning. Whatever you learn, you possess and claim as yours. If you learn gardening, the skill becomes yours; if you learn hairdressing, you acquire it and claim it as yours. You can even put a price tag on acquired skills.

Sometimes, when people do not seem to have certain knowledge, it is because they are not willing to learn, and you will pay the price for whatever you are not willing to learn.

Learning allows things to go smoothly and saves you from exploitation. Laziness to learn leads to bondage. You become endangered to be a slave of whatever you do not understand. Learning also saves you from being underpaid in life. Those who lack a certain qualification acquired through learning are at the bottom of the corporate world's food chain. Therefore, learning is empowerment.

Today's generation frowns at learning; it laughs at black graduates and gives stats about how many unemployed graduates are out there. However, I want to encourage you never to undermine learning and qualification. Be proud of your achievements, of the time you spent at tertiary sharpening your skill. That was not a waste of time. When God finally opens doors for you, those doors must find you worthy because you have applied yourself to knowledge.

The problem nowadays is people who celebrate those multibillionaires who are school dropouts. They do not tell you these people have other superior senses, such as entrepreneurial and innovative ones. Unfortunately, not everyone has those senses; otherwise, everyone would be an inventor or a business guru.

The importance of education is that it also provides some form of security. Education does not make people billionaires but builds a work ethic in them. Even though some people have degrees but are not employed, this does not mean education is useless. I love this movie entitled "Colombiana" about a young girl (Amandla) who wanted to be a hit-woman, but her uncle convinced her that killing people is not just about pulling the trigger. There are disciplines and skills one must learn in a classroom.

I never finished school. The only reason I make it in secular Babylon is that I have other senses working for me. Secondly, I never stop learning. Many things that people learn in a classroom I learn from YouTube. However, when government job opportunities come through, someone like me cannot apply. The system was designed to recognize people with qualifications, not just skills. It is a mistake for you to quit school or to quit learning.

## Through Reading

Reading is the cousin of learning; it means that I can still learn and grow in a certain field even if I did not have the opportunity to learn it in a classroom. Great leaders are great readers; never stop reading.

Reading is a discipline. The mind and body are not always willing to comply, but as a leader, you must always force yourself to read for you to lead successfully. To lead is to be ahead; to be ahead, you must read a lot. You could lead at home even if you are not the firstborn, in academia even if you do not have a Ph.D., in business even if you were not born with business genes, or in ministry even if you do not have big gifts.

Men and women who are successful leaders or ahead in their field must discipline their minds to learn. Sometimes that learning was not in a classroom but in the study room. I do not believe that research is a profession that always requires a qualification, such as journalism. I believe one can become a researcher by being a reader.

When you are a reader, you become aware of your surroundings. Reading much history makes you wise not to repeat past mistakes. If you read about business, you become wise in your dealings with money. Reading more about marriage and relationships makes you wise to be a good husband or wife. If you read more about psychology, you understand people better.

Nowadays, there is either a book or tutorial about everything. You can learn anything from the comfort of your home. There is no excuse for illiteracy in this time and age. Refuse to be a follower and become a reader. In religion, there is this tendency to warn people against reading certain books. For example, in Christianity, they will warn you against reading the Quran and vice versa. This is a bad way to go about life; if you are a Christian, read about Islam and other religions and test the truth of what you believe. This will put you in a position to defend your faith better.

I interact with many people on Tiktok who ask me difficult questions about my faith. I never answer those questions without doing proper research about the subject and reading about the sources from which they are arguing. This helps me to understand better where they are coming from.

We become friends with knowledge through reading. Reading is free and doable. Today there are libraries almost everywhere. You can also use apps and search engines to acquire more knowledge. There is a Nguni Christian term we use for someone speaking nonsense called "ihlathi." Ihlathi simply means this person is speaking confusion. There is no reason for ihlathi in your speech, presentation, or sermon. There is no room or excuse for any of that.

Some, through reading, found themselves becoming better speakers. They ended up earning through speaking. E.g., in the field of comedy, you can tell if a comedian is a reader, like Dave Chapelle or Trevor Noah. A comic who reads is usually on point concerning current events in their comedy. The same is true with preaching. Revelation and anointing are not enough; one needs to read as well.

### Through mentorship

Mentorship is also an extension of learning. In life, it is very important to have a mentor. A mentor is someone who has mastered a certain field or skill set, like a sensei, a priest, or a sangoma. These three are mentors. The sensei teaches martial arts, the priest teaches scripture/prayer, and the sangoma teaches divination.

A mentor is a teacher outside of a classroom; for example, your father is your mentor. By default, we learn many things at home. It is very crucial to find a mentor to grow in your skill. NOTE: When looking for a mentor, you sometimes have to pay for their help. You must be willing to pay someone for you to grow quicker in your potential. There are some things you cannot learn on your own. We are not wired the same way; for example, I cannot learn mathematics alone; I am very bad with calculations. If I needed to learn math, I would need a tutor.

**Through experience**

We gain experience through application; when we apply the little knowledge we have, we grow in experience, which gives us an advantage in life, such as in relationships or at the workplace. An experience is a form of wisdom and knowledge. There are certain things you cannot fully know without experiencing them yourself. Therefore, when you are afraid to try, you limit your experience, and it is difficult to trust someone without experience.

In the corporate world, education is not enough; one must have some years of experience. Having a driver's license is not enough; experience also counts. Experience is the most important part of learning. Some experiences are painful, and some are due to our faults and mistakes, but once you learn them, they are yours.

Success is measured by how you use an experience. Some people are destroyed by their experiences, and some empower therapists because of painful experiences. Some use their experiences as an excuse to harm others, and others as an excuse not to prosper. Some use their experiences to make money, start companies and ministries, and empower others.

Your experience can either make you or break you. Some allow their prison experience to lend them back to prison, and some use it to start an NPO. Your past can either render you poor or pay your bills.

Two people who were raped ten years ago may not both end up committing suicide; maybe one of them may become a millionaire. Both experiences are painful, but one may use their experience to empower others, write a book, start a talk show, and make money. This is an irony to me; it raises the question of what would have happened had they both not been raped? Would the former still commit suicide, and would the latter still become a millionaire?

Somehow, we cannot dismiss that our experiences influence us in one way or the other. We cannot ignore the fact that how one uses their experience counts. We can blame the suicide of the former on the rape, but we cannot ignore the fact that the latter's success is because of the same rape.

What are you doing with your experiences? Are you crafting them into a positive weapon like a blacksmith? Are you writing a proposal to the government using your painful experience as an entry point? Or are you crying and complaining that life is not fair? While you are contemplating hanging yourself, someone else is writing a bestseller. Do not kill yourself because of your painful experience; use it to heal others.

Acquired leadership is available for everyone from all walks of life. You may have been born in the poorest village, but you can become a leader through acquired sense. Yes, you can become the best at what you do. People who excel will end up drawing followers and disciples.

# THREE

# SUPERNATURAL SENSE

I am currently working on a book titled "Prophetic Intelligence." I learned throughout the years that there is a supernatural sense. This intelligence gives believers or spiritual (prophetic) people in the marketplace an advantage.

Before understanding the importance of having a supernatural sense, you must understand that leadership is spiritual or supernatural. No leader in politics or business does not have a form of spiritual/supernatural backup. Some leaders have gone to lengths spiritually to have the success they now have. Therefore, the Bible teaches us not to envy the success of the wicked because we do not know what this person has done to gain wealth and success.

If you are a believer in the marketplace, you need to understand the importance of your spirituality, namely, Biblical spirituality and how it works. Remember that, as a Christian, you are competing with those who serve other deities. They, too, have a gospel to preach through their success. When they are ahead of you, their gods receive glory. That's why worshippers of God were more successful in scripture than their enemies.

God made Abraham the richest man alive through the supernatural sense. Isaac was richer than all the Philistines combined. Jacob became richer than Laban while working for him. Joseph and Daniel were the wisest in their time; the list continues.

David represented the worship of Yahweh when he killed Goliath with a slingshot. In the marketplace, you compete with other religions and spiritualities. In Africa, Biblical Spirituality and African Spirituality are at odds with each other. Some subscribe to Biblical Spirituality in the workplace, and others follow African Spirituality. Let the God who answers by fire be God.

Leadership, success, and money are spiritual concepts. The older generation in African Spirituality understood that one must strengthen one's home, job, or marriage by invoking the spirits of the dead. We, believers consider this an abomination; however, the principle is the same. The principle is everything you do must have a spiritual backup.

David calls God his shield, fortress, refuge, and stronghold. All these words reveal that David had strengthened his kingdom through the worship of Yahweh. Anyone who frowns at spirituality lacks supernatural sense. Such a person is prone to fail when dealing with an opposition that uses some spiritual power or witchcraft.

Successful leaders understand that there must be some spiritual sacrifices to invoke supernatural intervention. Even those millionaires that are not "that spiritual" give alms. They unwitting apply a universal Biblical principle, and God is bound by His Word to bless them.

To ignore the spiritual element of successful leadership is to set yourself up for failure. Supernatural sense is the ability to connect to the spiritual realm to manipulate physical events. It is tapping into the unseen to remote-control the seen. It is the potential to walk in the unknown world to dominate in the known world.

Jesus was not a politician; He was not educated, He had no acquired sense, and He was not a businessman, but He used His supernatural proclivity to make an impact on the earth. His supernatural sense raised the dead, healed the sick, walked on water, and raised Him from the dead. It was His supernatural sense alone that gave Him His success.

We see this even in indigenous cults and faiths. People in our villages have become prominent leaders in the supernatural sense. My father was a prominent leader in the Jericho church; he gained prominence through nothing but a supernatural sense. He was not a man of special skill or education but influenced hundreds of lives through his spirituality. He raised us without medical aid or insurance; he depended solely on his spirituality. His spirituality was not Biblical, but I learned from him that there is a supernatural realm and that we can draw from it.

There is nothing scientific about a medium or diviner. Mediums have supernatural senses and use them to serve their communities and feed their families. When dealing with success, we cannot ignore the supernatural as a serious aspect. In my former book titled "The Apostolic And Prophetic Prayer Manual," I present the importance of prayer and fasting because I believe that success in any field does not just happen; someone must pray and fast.

I advocate for Biblical spirituality as a clean, unadulterated source for the supernatural sense. Faith in the Lord Jesus Christ is not just for going to heaven, but it carries tremendous power for daily living. The Christian faith has always been synonymous with supernatural power. This supernatural power was not only spiritual but also intangible. The Bible teaches that believers have this power, allowing them to do things others cannot do. This power allows Christians to do the following supernaturally:

Heal the sick.

Perform miracles.

Raise the dead.

Speak prophetic words.

Speak words of knowledge and wisdom.

Have inhumane faith.

Discern thoughts, intentions, and spirits.

Speak unknown, new languages and interpret.

Cast out evil spirits.

From this, we can see how tremendous this power is. Believers in Christ have the Holy Spirit; the Holy Spirit is called three major things in Isaiah 11:2, which are:

The Spirit of Wisdom and Understanding

The Spirit of Counsel and Might

The Spirit of Knowledge and the Fear of the Lord.

Believers have all this at their disposal; when they spend more time praying, fasting, and reading scriptures, they allow these gifts and powers to flow. In every comic book or movie, every hero has a special power. Did you know that believers are superheroes? Yes, they have superpowers.

You may have been born in poverty but have a superpower unlike anything you have seen before. You are a superhero, and the enemy does not want you to know that.

## Common Sense Vs Supernatural Sense

Common sense plans; supernatural sense prays.

Common sense is developed through maturation; supernatural sense is received through impartation.

Common sense gathers money; supernatural sense scatters money.

Common sense sees possibilities through deductive reasoning; supernatural sense speaks possibilities through faith.

Common sense is natural; supernatural sense is spiritual.

Common sense is buying and selling; supernatural sense is giving and receiving.

Common sense is earthly wisdom; supernatural sense is heavenly wisdom.

Common sense depends on how much money a person has; supernatural sense depends on how much faith one has.

Common sense is limited by the economy; supernatural sense is limited by one's faith.

Poverty, according to common sense, is the absence of money; poverty, according to supernatural sense, is the absence of ideas.

Common sense avoids risks; supernatural sense takes risks.

Common sense believes after seeing; supernatural sense believes before seeing.

Common sense is logical; supernatural sense is spiritual.

Common sense plans on a budget; supernatural sense plans on faith.

Common sense is applauded; supernatural sense is laughed at.

I can assure you that many great men had to apply supernatural sense at times and defy common sense rules. It was a laughable matter when Jesus told the mourners that the child was not dead but asleep, but they were soon silenced when the child came to life. The same is true with the four men who opened the house's roof where Jesus was teaching and brought down a paralytic. Their faith was a laughable matter. They defied common sense.

Peter went against common sense when he listened to Jesus when He said, "launch into the deep." Such a statement was laughable, but he had to apply supernatural sense. Men and women of supernatural sense are crazy until what they say comes to pass. Supernatural sense is for leaders. Those who will lead in this life need to be a little crazy to see the impossible coming to pass.

### Laws Of Applying Supernatural Sense

One must thoroughly hear God; what the Lord says, He backs. Faith is not a decision, but it is an activation. It is an endowment that is activated when someone hears God properly. Acting in a supernatural sense is not a random thing. We apply faith from a position of conviction.

Faith is not positive thinking or the power of the mind, it is total dependence on God's Word and the leading of the Holy Spirit. The Lord leads us into the things we believe Him for; because we have heard His promise, we trust His faithfulness.

Therefore, faith is a response to an intimate relationship between man and God. The relationship is both theological and experiential.

Secondly, one must take time in prayer [and probably fasting] before acting out in a supernatural sense. If need be, one must wait for other prophets to confirm before applying.

One can also use common sense to apply supernatural sense. This means it is common sense to apply supernatural sense where common sense has failed. Suppose you are a hard worker and qualified for a certain position, yet you keep getting bypassed; it is common sense to recognize that there might be a spiritual or demonic manipulation behind your problem. You do not need to be a prophet to at least suspect that supernatural intervention is needed.

Another example is if you are a married couple and you have tried everything medically possible to conceive, yet nothing happens, it is common sense to at least try supernatural means. For some, these means may involve an extra-biblical effort, such as going to a traditional healer but for us who are saved and believe, we turn to prayer and fasting. The point is, do not give up before trying the paranormal.

If all you have is Western medicine and answers, I mourn for you. You need something beyond science to get results where science has failed. If your faith ends with science, you are limiting yourself, and there are other dimensions of leadership and influence you will never experience.

The application of supernatural sense is according to faith and faith alone. Therefore, one must not waver in faith when applying supernatural sense. The willingness to defy the laws of logic is sometimes the only key to greatness.

# FOUR

# ENTREPRENEURIAL SENSE

In this chapter, we will use the term "entrepreneur" to discuss a variety of fields and not just business. We are looking at achieving a certain quality of an entrepreneurial leader. The entrepreneurial leader is not simply a pioneer in business but in other endeavors. This means that the same quality general entrepreneurs have must be seen in every leader. We will learn to achieve those qualities by developing an entrepreneurial sense/mindset.

According to Meriam Webster's Dictionary an entrepreneur is a person who starts a business and is willing to risk a loss to make money. It also says it is someone who organizes, manages, and assumes the risks of business and enterprise.

Entrepreneurs are pioneers and visionaries; they are not just businesspeople but visionaries. They are willing to risk it all on an idea with the hopes of making a profit.

Entrepreneurial sense is also supernatural in that the entrepreneur operates by faith in an idea or product. Entrepreneurs are not only found in business but also politics and ministry. It takes entrepreneurial sense to pioneer anything from the ground up and believe in it enough to lay down your life to make sure it happens.

The entrepreneurial sense has the following qualities:

**The ability to see the outcome before implementation.** All successful leaders can see what others do not see; they can envision the end from the beginning. Whatever they do is in line with the end they have in mind. Entrepreneurs' vision informs them how to pioneer their work and manage it.

**The ability to have the courage to start amid fear.** Entrepreneurs are very courageous. It takes extreme courage to lead and to be successful.

They take risks not because they are fearless but because they are courageous.

People are usually afraid of the following:

1. THEY FEAR THE UNKNOWN. They are afraid of not knowing what will happen once they start. Entrepreneurs also fear the unknown; however, they also imagine the unknown and believe it shall be as they desire.

2. THEY FEAR FAILURE. The fear of failure is failure itself because it deprives you of proper growth and experience. The fear of failure is usually born out of past failures or the failures of others. One is afraid of getting married because of a past failed marriage. This fear can kill the desire for one to try. Many people are afraid to initiate anything because of this fear. It cripples one's creative abilities. Entrepreneurs use that fear as a motivator to work hard and diligently.

3. THEY FEAR EMBARRASSMENT. Another dangerous feeling that follows failure is a shame. Shame is more dangerous than sin itself. It keeps people from fixing their lives after they fall or fail. We do not know why Ronda Rousey quit the UFC after losing to Holly Holms, but it might be because she was embarrassed. Shame can cause you to abort something that would have made you a great success. Again, the entrepreneurial mindset is important because it

allows you to use that fear as fuel to the fire. It helps to make one work harder than to quit.

I want to encourage you not to be afraid. Go for your dreams and ignore the negative past and reports of others. Leaders are not made of what they know theoretically but of what has worked for them.

Leading men and women are not immune to fear and doubt but have an attitude that allows them to thrive amid the doubt and fear.

**The ability to pave the way for others.** Entrepreneurs are deliverers; they can lead others to freedom. When entrepreneurs take the necessary risks to pioneer a business or a project, they unwittingly allow others to work and earn a living for themselves.

Entrepreneurs are today's Moses leaders; they lift whole nations from the bondage of poverty through the risks they take. Entrepreneurship is not for the selfish but for those who believe in empowering others.

Those who have entrepreneurial intelligence are trailblazers. They are the architects of apostolic building concepts and set the tone for others to mold their lives, businesses, and projects after; they are trendsetters.

**The ability to manage.** Management determines whether something will last or not. How one manages a car, house, ministry, or relationship determines if it will have longevity. Entrepreneurs are wise managers of goods and funds. They are not wasters of money and time, but they act according to the goal they have in mind.

An entrepreneurial mindset is necessary to become effective in leadership. One cannot lead well if they have poor administrative skills. Entrepreneurial sense deals with proper structures for the organization to function well.

**The ability to realistically look at the world without judgment.** This point is also why religious people never make it as entrepreneurs. Church people see the world almost the same as academic people. They feel the need to comment on why things are how they are. On the other hand, entrepreneurs have a certain level of cynicism and indifference. Entrepreneurs will see the horrible things that happen worldwide and think of how to make money from them.

Cynicism is also a little bit scriptural. A cynic sees people for what they are, and to some level, the Bible teaches us to be cynical (for lack of a better word). You cannot lead people if you don't understand human psychology. The entrepreneurial sense understands humans and how they think.

You see, the Bible teaches that humans are evil. It says the heart is desperately wicked, and we should not trust humans. All those are cynical ways of seeing the world. It turns out that what we call cynical is realistic - an accurate depiction of humans.

Naivety limits your effectiveness. You cannot lead well if you don't understand what humans are capable of. Entrepreneurs are not delusional; they are aware of their world, which puts them in a better position to lead effectively.

**The ability to aggressively and sometimes ruthlessly get things done without being unethical.** As a believer who wants to win in the world, you first need to learn that nice is not a fruit of the Spirit. Being ethical is not the same as being nice. People who have an entrepreneurial sense are not necessarily nice, but they are always ethical. Being nice is a horrible quality in leadership; a nice king can never become a great king. A nice businessperson can never become great. Firmness is part of leadership.

Sometimes to get things done as a leader, you need to be more like a midwife. A midwife only cares about the unborn baby, not the mother's feelings during delivery. If the midwife is too concerned about the mother's feelings, the baby might get hurt along the way.

A scientist or leader in the sciences cannot effectively lead this generation if he is nice. This is because we live in a world where feelings matter above facts. Today there will be laws that carter for and protect the feelings of certain people or groups even if what they are protecting is scientifically, morally, and spiritually incorrect. One cannot be a leader if they are politically correct and super nice.

In a world where truth is labeled hate speech, one cannot lead unless they are firm. That firmness may lead to cancellation and imprisonment, but entrepreneurial leaders are risk-takers.

**The ability to turn a disadvantage into an advantage.** The best entrepreneurs are always conscious of their limitations and shortcomings. One professor made an example between a lion and a rabbit and said that a rabbit is more likely to live long because it knows where it belongs in the food chain. On the other hand, the lion is not too concerned about danger because it knows that no predator can harm it in the animal food chain.

The rabbit can use its fear to survive; it is more aware of its surroundings than the lion.

Entrepreneurs can use a setback and turn it into a comeback. They can make a profit from a sad story. I made an example of rape and how someone else can turn that sad reality into profit.

A leader with an entrepreneurial mindset sees opportunities within disabilities. Entrepreneurial leaders are always hungry to learn; they never act as if they have arrived in life. They have the fear of a rabbit, not the complacency of a lion. This makes them easily recognize their limitations and find ways to turn them around and profit from them.

## Can Anyone Become An Entrepreneur?

Entrepreneurship is not a personality type or for certain people; we can all be pioneers. We can all be leaders if we are willing to take the steps and the risks. I want you to know that leaders are not born, nor are they a gene type. It is the willingness to take the steps no one is willing to take.

As aforementioned, an entrepreneur is willing to take risks to pioneer a project on earth. Anyone with an idea unique to them is a potential entrepreneur.

## The Entrepreneurial Mindset Is Scriptural

There is one quality I have learned about as I did some research for this book. When I first learned of this quality, I was surprised, but the more I followed up on it, the more I found it to be interesting and very scriptural.

This quality is, all successful entrepreneurs are insecure. Yes, you heard me correctly; I was also blown away when I learned this. The quality that successful entrepreneurs have is what motivational speakers teach us to get rid of. For most of my life, I have been trying hard to be more confident and believe in myself. However, after learning about entrepreneurs' insecurities, I realized that "believing in yourself" is not even scriptural.

Apparently, entrepreneurs have been scriptural all the time. If you look at all the heroes in the Bible, their confidence was never in themselves. It was always in the Lord. They could face all odds because they trusted their God and not because they believed in themselves.

Look at most successful people and see how paranoid some of them are. They sleep for three hours and spend most of their time perfecting their craft. While the poor and middle class are relaxed, watching Bollywood movies, entrepreneurs are up late, making sure everything is in order.

This paranoia renders people great; most billionaires are not that attractive, and some are not even educated. It seems the lack of qualification sometimes is the qualification needs to succeed. Abraham's wife was barren, Hannah was barren, Mary, the mother of the Lord, was from Nazareth (yikes), and Jephthah was the son of a prostitute.

Paul called himself the "least of the apostles," yet he wrote more books, preached in more places, and planted more churches. Some of the most deserving apostles did almost nothing that we know of. We see another story of the daughters of Zelophehad who protested for their father's land at a time when the laws of the land did not favor them (Numbers 27: 1-5). It seems that even God has always used the misfits to do great things.

The same could be said about women pastors; since there are divisions in the Body about whether they should lead churches or not, they seem to become more successful in the ministry than most men. Secondly, the many scandals of sexual immorality are hardly found among women preachers.

I find this interesting; disadvantage can be a tool for greatness. Ahimahaz ran faster than the Ethiopian messenger even though Joab prohibited him. David ended up killing a lion, bear, and some giants even though his family rejected him. Melchizedek came from the Jebusites, who were lame or blind, yet he became the priest of God Most High and blessed Abraham. How Melchizedek achieved such a status from a cursed nation is beyond me.

Jesus is the "stone that the builders rejected," yet He became the "chief cornerstone." How did He pull that off? All these great men and women had one thing in common; they did not have faith in themselves. They perceived themselves as inadequate and unworthy, and so they fought hard to be worthy. In the Biblical sense, they turned to the One who could perfect them, namely, God the Father.

Insecurity can be toxic, but it can also be weaponized against failure. An insecure wife can destroy or improve her marriage by doing extra work. An insecure husband can become abusive or improve the quality of his marriage by putting in extra work.

Being secure is good if one is secure on something real, not a façade. For example, some people trust in their money, some in their spouses, and some in their adequacy or qualification. That, in turn, can produce a sense of entitlement and complacency. Most people who feel secure are often complacent and end up being unproductive.

This type of insecurity is met with security in something real, viz. God. That security does not give birth to complacency but hard work. A pastor who trusts in his gift, anointing, or training will never put in the same effort as another put who trust in the Lord. It is only the sense of security found in God that leads to exploits. The fall of Jerusalem in Jeremiah's time came from a false sense of security, leading to people not working on their lives and fixing what was wrong.

Entrepreneurial leadership is never complacent. Such leaders never reach a place where they think they have arrived. They are always growing and pushing.

# FIVE

# INNOVATIVE SENSE

Leaders are innovators and can think up new things and methods. This sense is important because, without innovations, there can never be any progress. We would still be stuck in the Stone Age if it was not for people who came up with innovations.

Inventions make the world a better place. When people say they miss the good old days, I believe they mean that morally and socially because technologically, the world is better now than fifty years ago. These new technologies have brought in new eras on earth. Without innovative leaders, there can never be development.

Through creativity, life has become better in different areas. Cooking has become easier and more enjoyable because of those who came up with inventions in the kitchen. Transportation has become more convenient because of the invention of better modes of transportation, such as cars and airplanes. The same is true with communication; civilization has moved from sending a raven to sending a WhatsApp message.

The world becomes better and nicer with new inventions. I was thinking about the Great Commission the other day, how going to all the world for years meant booking a flight to that place. Little did we know that we would reach countless people years later through a cellphone. The world may be morally corrupt, but it is the best time to be alive, all because of innovation.

## God, The Greatest Inventor

One of the titles of God is Creator; He is the One who thought up this universe. Therefore, creativity is a divine gift that bears witness to our being made in God's image. Without creativity, the world as we know it would not exist.

I believe that when the scripture says God has put eternity in the hearts of men, it also refers to creativity. We can invent stuff because we are all children of the Father as far as creation is concerned.

Understanding God as the Creator is not just religious but a powerful position. It reveals what we, as humans, can do. To believe in evolution and natural selection and not creation also insinuates that there is no such thing as creativity because whatever people invent, they are predisposed to do so. In other words, they were not free to develop those inventions.

The belief in creativity suggests that one also believes in free thinking and free will. One cannot believe in that unless they believe in the Biblical God. This means that since our God is the Creator, He has imparted the ability to be creative to us.

Since we were created in the image and likeness of God, we carry some level of creative thoughts and ideas. Many people are not exploring their creativity, so I have included this chapter. God is raising believers and releasing them into the marketplace.

One of the areas believers need to start occupying is the creative field. Christians have been active throughout history in contributing to new sciences, medicine, and academia. However, it seems that many Christians have become complacent and are content with only being spiritually relevant. God is now calling His people to use their brains and invent.

## The Vocation Of Invention

I believe that creativity can be a vocation. God is calling prophets and wise men who will infiltrate secular Babylon and lead through inventions. It is not just scientific and technological to invent, but also a scriptural thing.

In Isaiah, God promises that He is doing a new thing. In the Book of Acts, He promises times of refreshing. One of the gifts of the Spirit deals with newness. Tongues are called "new tongues." Believers are promised the ability to speak new languages through the Spirit, languages they have never learned. If the Spirit can impart new languages, what other new thing can He impart?

Creativity is our heritage as believers. For one to invent something, they must first see it in the spirit. For one to see in the spirit, they must be a seer. Therefore, I present to you that inventors are seers. Unlike prophecy, being a seer is genetic; one can grow up with seeing abilities.

Others believe in what they see in their minds, and others don't. Those who take what they see seriously do great exploits on the earth. What do you see? Jeremiah's ministry began with the question, "What do you see?" What you see can be the beginning of your prophetical, political, or entrepreneurial career.

Many years ago, I saw words. I wrote down those words, and they turned into notes, notes turned into manuals, manuals turned into books, books turned into publications, and publications turned into sales. Your small idea can turn you into an entrepreneur. Your idea can employ and empower other people.

The publisher and the editor fully depend on the creativity of the writer. When your mind is blocked as a writer, someone's bills are delayed from being paid. Your lack of creativity is unemployment for someone. While others blame the government for the lack of jobs, I blame you. You and your lazy mind are the worst pandemics the world has ever seen.

Inventions are cures, both literally and figuratively. Some diseases are said to be incurable, but the truth is that no one has produced a cure yet. Some situations will remain unsolved because someone, somewhere, whom God had appointed to be the solution is lazy to think.

### God's Creative Spirit Has Been Poured On All Flesh

Interestingly, the Spirit of wisdom is the one Spirit that operates even upon unbelievers and atheists. It does not discriminate; I believe this is because the world cannot move forward without someone thinking of something new. Therefore,

God has made it so that even those who deny Him will operate in His creative power. Therefore, wisdom is not in the godliness equation but in the thinking equation.

Believers are beneficiaries of many inventions by unbelievers. Looking at Tiktok today, I am grateful because I can reach thousands with the Gospel, yet an unbeliever might have invented it. In this, I see the genius of God.

Out of the seven mountains of influence [Zion being the first], wisdom is not restricted to the first mountain, viz. Zion. Zion is the home of wisdom, yet Zion people are not exhibiting her traits. The church is displaying power and not wisdom. This is because wisdom is not sought as anointing/power is sought.

One can fast and pray for power, but wisdom is trickier than that. Even though wisdom in a certain area can be released through prayer that is a facet of wisdom. True creative wisdom is sought through how we apply our minds to it. What do I mean? Wisdom/creativity comes whenever there is a need for a solution. To have a solution, one must think it out. Therefore, wisdom is not in the prayer equation but in the thinking equation.

An intercessor can pray for a cure, but the answer will come from an actual doctor who can think in that capacity. Christians can pray for solutions, but thinkers will receive the answers unless those same Christians become thinkers.

God will give wisdom to thinkers and not intercessors. Believers need to upgrade into becoming thinkers as well.

### The Thinking Mind

The thinking mind is the only thing standing between us and total anarchy. It is the only thing that separates us from animals. Yet even so, the average human uses 10-20% of his brain. What would happen if there were humans who used at least 50%?

We saw what happened with Christ; He utilized all His brain. He was the wisest Man who ever lived. The mind that thinks of new things brings an evolution. The evolution that comes from innovation brings a revolution. Revolutionaries are great leaders who destabilize the matrix.

All these systems, namely, education, religion etc. are part of an established matrix that sometimes keeps people from thinking for themselves. Failure to utilize your mind on fundamental issues also kills one's creativity.

The thinking mind is sometimes mistaken for a rebellious mind because it destabilizes the matrix. Yet, even so, it is the Neos of the world who challenge the matrix who bring real change in society. If we all follow the same thinking pattern, we will not bring true change to our generation.

The world needs thinkers. It needs people who refuse to conform to this world's standards but who bring the world to a new way with renewed minds. Sometimes the new way is the original way before the matrix took over. I encourage you to keep thinking and asking questions because the whole world will stop moving forward without you.

## This Can Be Learned

Innovation gives you an advantage so that even if you were not formerly educated, you can still become a leading man or woman. Innovation is not always about technological inventions; it is about people who can think outside the box. The world needs such people.

Therefore, innovation is not just a special gift that is unique to certain people, but I believe it is something that can be developed; you can develop an innovative reflex or muscle memory. When it comes to wealth creation sometimes, you need to be a Joseph and think of solutions that no one is thinking about. You need to be a Daniel and bring realities no one knew were possible such as telling people their dreams and interpretation.

Thinkers push the boundaries of what society thinks is possible. Innovation is a supernatural practice; it is not a Christian practice but a supernatural one. For lack of better words, I can say that innovative people are mediums, diviners, seers, or prophets. Oh yes, they can convey to men what is beyond the curtain of the mind.

Innovators do not have to be highly intelligent people. They often fail at school; they are not the brightest and smartest. However, they become leaders because they can imagine what no one can think about.

## ABOUT THE AUTHOR

Nicholas Dlamini is an apostle of Jesus Christ whom God has called to preach, teach, and demonstrate the Word of Life in this generation. He was born in Eswatini Lobamba Lomdzala and now lives in Boekenhouthoek KwaNdebele, South Africa.

His ministry is strictly apostolic and prophetic empowerment through books and online platforms. He currently serves under the leadership of Dr PM and Apostle T. Mashiye.

He currently runs the INTENSE WORD SESSIONS on Facebook, WhatsApp, YouTube, and Tiktok, where he teaches the Word.

www.ingramcontent.com/pod-product-compliance
Lightning Source LLC
Chambersburg PA
CBHW021918040426
42448CB00007B/812